First World War
and Army of Occupation
War Diary
France, Belgium and Germany

36 DIVISION
Divisional Troops
154 Brigade Royal Field Artillery
26 November 1915 - 31 August 1916

WO95/2496/4

The Naval & Military Press Ltd
www.nmarchive.com
Published in association with The National Archives

Published by

The Naval & Military Press Ltd

Unit 10 Ridgewood Industrial Park,

Uckfield, East Sussex,

TN22 5QE England

Tel: +44 (0) 1825 749494

www.naval-military-press.com

www.nmarchive.com

This diary has been reprinted in facsimile from the original. Any imperfections are inevitably reproduced and the quality may fall short of modern type and cartographic standards.

© **Crown Copyright**
Images reproduced by permission of The National Archives, London, England, 2015.

Contents

Document type	Place/Title	Date From	Date To
Heading	WO95/2496/4		
Heading	36th Division 154th Brigade R.F.A. 1915 Nov Dec 1915-Aug 1916		
Heading	154e Bde RFA Vol I		
Miscellaneous	From OC 154 Bde RFA	20/02/1916	20/02/1916
War Diary	Bordon	26/11/1915	27/11/1915
War Diary	Southampton	27/11/1915	27/11/1915
War Diary	Havre	01/12/1915	04/12/1915
War Diary	Cocquerel	05/12/1915	05/12/1915
War Diary	Francieres	05/12/1915	05/12/1915
War Diary	Cocquerel Francieres	12/12/1915	23/01/1916
War Diary	Cayeux S/Mer	24/01/1916	24/02/1916
War Diary	Pernois	02/02/1916	03/02/1916
War Diary	St. Oven.	14/02/1916	14/02/1916
War Diary	Pernois	24/02/1916	24/02/1916
War Diary	Puchvillers	26/02/1916	26/02/1916
War Diary	Cayeux S M	25/02/1916	25/02/1916
War Diary	Pontremy	26/02/1916	28/02/1916
War Diary	Pernois	29/02/1916	29/02/1916
War Diary	Louvencourt	01/03/1916	01/03/1916
War Diary	Bertrancourt	04/03/1916	04/03/1916
War Diary	Forceville	05/03/1916	05/03/1916
War Diary	Orville	12/03/1916	12/03/1916
War Diary	Mailly Mallet	02/03/1916	03/03/1916
War Diary	Martinsart	02/03/1916	10/03/1916
War Diary	Mailly Maillet	14/03/1916	18/03/1916
War Diary	Martinsart	19/03/1916	19/03/1916
War Diary	Mailly-Maillet	20/03/1916	23/03/1916
War Diary	Martinsart	25/03/1916	26/03/1916
War Diary	Mailly Maillet	30/03/1916	02/04/1916
War Diary	Forceville	02/04/1916	05/04/1916
War Diary	Martinsart	02/04/1916	17/04/1916
War Diary	Forceville	18/04/1916	18/04/1916
War Diary	Martinsart	18/04/1916	21/05/1916
War Diary	Forceville	01/05/1916	25/05/1916
War Diary	Harponville	22/05/1916	26/05/1916
War Diary	Mesnil	21/05/1916	21/05/1916
War Diary	Martinsart	31/05/1916	31/05/1916
War Diary	Mesnil	01/07/1916	06/07/1916
War Diary	Thiepval Wood	04/07/1916	04/07/1916
War Diary	Aveloy Wood	08/07/1916	08/07/1916
War Diary	Mesnil	09/07/1916	09/07/1916
War Diary	Albert	07/07/1916	12/07/1916
War Diary	Forceville	14/07/1916	14/07/1916
War Diary	Autheville	15/07/1916	15/07/1916
War Diary	Conchy	16/07/1916	16/07/1916
War Diary	Monchy	17/07/1916	17/07/1916
War Diary	Delette	18/07/1916	18/07/1916
War Diary	Clerques	19/07/1916	19/07/1916
War Diary	St Omer	20/07/1916	20/07/1916

War Diary	Courte Croix	21/07/1916	21/07/1916
War Diary	Wulverghem	21/07/1916	27/07/1916
War Diary	Locre	31/07/1916	31/07/1916
War Diary	Ploegsteert	01/08/1916	01/08/1916
War Diary	Wulverghem	01/08/1916	03/08/1916
War Diary	White Gates	05/08/1916	16/08/1916
War Diary	Dranoutre	16/08/1916	27/08/1916
War Diary	Wulverghem	27/08/1916	31/08/1916
Heading	WO95/Stray/NNN		

WO 95/2496/K

36TH DIVISION

154TH BRIGADE R.F.A.
1915 Nov ~~DEC 1915~~-AUG 1916

BROKEN UP

36TH DIVISION

From O.C. 152 Bde R.F.A.
To O/C A.G's Office,
   Base.

Enclosed herewith War Diary completed as desired to send for January last.

The reason I requested you to cancel the former War Diary, is that it was not signed by me, & was not completed & was forwarded in error. F C Johnston
LT. COL. COMDG.
152 BRIGADE R.F.A.

In the Field.
20.2.16.

Army Form C. 2118

WAR DIARY
or
INTELLIGENCE SUMMARY
(Erase heading not required.)

154th (HOW.) Bde. R.F.A.
51st Division

Place	Date	Hour	Summary of Events and Information	Remarks and references to Appendices
BORDON	26/11/15	5.30 pm	Am. Col. 154 Bde R.F.A. left for SOUTHAMPTON DOCKS in FRANCE 28/11/15	
"	27/11/15	-	H.Q. & Batteries arrived SOUTHAMPTON DOCKS	
SOUTHAMPTON	27/11/15		Embarked on S.S. "N.W. MILLER" & HAVRE. During night engine broke down - returned to SOLENT & lay off there all 28/11/15 - started again evening 28/11/15 - break down reported, returned again. Disembarked guns - explsn the "S.S." "N.W. MILLER" & mashoped every thing new morning the S.S. "NIRVANA"	
HAVRE	1/12/15		Arrived at 7 am off HAVRE after a rough passage. Disembarked & were away by 12 midnight to Rest Camp I.	
"	1/12/15–4pm		Entrained at HAVRE & arrived at PONTREMY 8.30 am 3/12/15	
COCQUEREL	3/12/15	-	After unloading marched to billets at COCQUEREL. H.Q. A & D batteries & Am. Col. billeted " B & C batteries billeted at FRANCIERES	
FRANCIERES COCQUEREL FRANCIERES	12/12/15 8/1/16		Commenced building horse standings. Finished 8/1/16	
"	23/1/16		The whole Brigade (less Am. Col.) moved to new area at PERNOIS. Am. Col moved to PERNOIS	
CAYEUX S/MER	24 & 31st January		Brigade (less Am. Col.) in billets at CAYEUX S/MER Am. Col. (with Bde in billets) at PERNOIS	

F.C. Johnson
LT. COL. COMDg.
154 BRIGADE R.F.A.

Army Form C. 2118

15th Howr. Bde R.F.A
Ulster Division
Commanded by Lt. Col. F. Campbell Johnston R.A.

WAR DIARY
or
INTELLIGENCE SUMMARY
(Erase heading not required.)

Instructions regarding War Diaries and Intelligence Summaries are contained in F.S. Regs., Part II. and the Staff Manual respectively. Title Pages will be prepared in manuscript.

Place	Date 1916	Hour	Summary of Events and Information	Remarks and references to Appendices
CAYEUX S/MER	Feby 1st/6/24th		Bde HQ & 4 Batteries at CAYEUX S/MER. Batteries carrying out firing practice.	
PERNOIS	Febry 2nd	19 - 23rd 6.30	Amn Column at PERNOIS	
"	3/2/16		" " leave for ST OUEN arriving same day.	
ST OUEN	14/2/16		" " " " PERNOIS " "	
PERNOIS	24/2/16		" " " " PUCHVILLERS " "	
PUCHVILLERS	28/2/16		" " " " LOUVENCOURT " "	
CAYEUX S/M	25/2/16		Bde HQ & 4 Batteries move by road to PONT-REMY. March I move owing to severe recent storm	
PONT-REMY	26/2/16		" " " "	
"	27/2/16		" " " "	
"	28/2/16		Bde HQ, B, C & D Batteries move by road to PERNOIS. A Bty moves by road to RENAULT FARM N. of BERNACOURT to join the 46th Division.	
PERNOIS	29/2/16		Bde HQ B, C & D Batteries move by road to LOUVENCOURT.	

F.C. Johnston
LT. COL. COMDG.
154 BRIGADE R.F.A.

Army Form C. 2118

WAR DIARY
—or—
INTELLIGENCE SUMMARY
(Erase heading not required.)

154. Bde R.F.A. (Howitzer)
36th Divisional Artillery
Commanded by Lt. Col. J.O. Johnston

Instructions regarding War Diaries and Intelligence Summaries are contained in F. S. Regs., Part II. and the Staff Manual respectively. Title Pages will be prepared in manuscript.

Place	Date March	Hour	Summary of Events and Information	Remarks and references to Appendices
LOUVENCOURT	1st	9 am	Bde H.Q., B, C & D Batteries & Ammunition Column billeted at LOUVENCOURT.	
BERTRANCOURT	4th	10.30am	B.A.C. Leave LOUVENCOURT for BERTRANCOURT	
FORCEVILLE	5th	8.30am	B.A.C. " BERTRANCOURT " FORCEVILLE	
ORVILLE	12th	9 am	B.A.C. " FORCEVILLE " ORVILLE	
MAILLY-MAILLET	2nd		C Battery staff digging a new position near MAILLY-MAILLET railway station	
"	3rd	9.30pm	Bde H.Q. Leave LOUVENCOURT for MAILLY-MAILLET & BERTRANCOURT	
MARTINSART	2nd		C Battery ordered to take over position from D/164 near MARTINSART to stop digging new position.	
"	7th	7 pm	Reg'l. position R C/154 taken over from D/164 in the evening	
"	8th	7.30pm	Left " " One gun from D/164 through N.O.2 gun - wise - action	
"	9th	4.30pm	C/154 retaliated on THIEPVAL. Gun - licked - mortars	
"	10th	11/45	" " " " " "	
MAILLY-MAILLET	14th	10.7am	Heavy hostile firing from 11am to 12.30am C/154 fire 62 rounds into THIEPVAL VILLAGE B/154 open fire on enemy cases at R.19.a.91 in German front line trench 3 direct hits on cap.	
"	17th	4.15 pm	D/154 fired 11 rounds of H.E. into REDAN at Q.5.a. our infantry having asked for retaliation	
"	18th	4.40pm	B/154 report having rain cust on yellowish tint (apparently from gas) steaming from trees, or from flames in the enemy's trenches - the wind not being favorable it ceased in a few minutes	
"	"	11.00am	D/154 Brigade called for retaliation. 15" H.E. shells were fired into enemy trenches at HAWTHORN REDOUBT	
MARTINSART	19th	9 pm	C/154 retaliated on Kratz trench mortar – ow trenches over Chaulier, owing to Flanders (Gen. Coleman) wounded	
MAILLYMAILLET	20th	3pm	B/154 fired 15 rounds into Kratz trench Kratz @ Q.18 C + Q.24 B.	
"	23rd	3.55pm	D/154 at request of infantry retaliated on Kratz trench mortar north of BEAUMONT. Enemy thin patrolled & pushed in front of BUCHONVILLERS.	
MARTINSART	25th	4.30	Hostile aeroplane dropped 4 bombs near MARTINSART	
"	26th	9 pm	C/154 at request of infantry retaliated on German trenches with 12 H.E. shells	
MAILLY-MAILLET	30th		B/154 report hostile aeroplane very active during morning	
"	31st		Quiet day	

E. Reading Lt. Col.
LT. COL. COMDr.
for 154 BRIGADE R.F.A.

154 RFA Vol 4
6

Army Form C. 2118

WAR DIARY
or
INTELLIGENCE SUMMARY
(Erase heading not required.)

154th Army Brigade R.F.A.
36th Divisional Artillery
Commanded by Lt. Col. F.C. Johnston R.F.A.

Instructions regarding War Diaries and Intelligence Summaries are contained in F.S. Regs., Part II. and the Staff Manual respectively. Title Pages will be prepared in manuscript.

Place	Date APRIL	Hour	Summary of Events and Information	Remarks and references to Appendices
MAILLY-MAILLET	1st		Quiet day. II/154 fired on a train in BEAUMONT STATION. Gun positions taken over by 31st Division.	
"	2nd		75 and 18 batteries move to FORCEVILLE in Reserve.	
FORCEVILLE	4th	2.30pm	Brigade H.Q. move from MAILLY-MAILLET to FORCEVILLE	
"	5th	9.30am	Bde Ammunition Column move to FORCEVILLE from LOUVENCOURT	
"	"		2/Lt Col MORRISON attached to 0/154 from Bde Am. Col.	
MARTINSART	3rd		ENEMY shell MESNIL and MARTINSART in flashes on returning from O.P.	
"	5th		0/154 fire into BEAUCOURT	
"	6th		Quiet day	
"	7th	9pm	Very heavy artillery in HAMEL Sector. C/154 opened fire on the road from MESNIL very hard fired 125 rounds	
"	"	10.30pm	Hostile artillery fire into MESNIL CHATEAU. C/154 retaliated on BEAUCOURT.	
"	8th		Lt H.A.G. WALTON joined C/154. Quiet day	
"	9th		Quiet day	
"	10th		C/154 fired 16 rounds in retaliation & 12 rounds at ST PIERRE - DIVION	
"	11,12,13,14th		Quiet days	
"	15th	12 mid. night	C/154 fired 30 rounds on trenches in ST PIERRE DIVION, barn in BEAUCOURT STATION	
"	16th		C/154 fired 16 rounds in THIEPVAL CHATEAU	
"	17th		C/154 Crews dug-out in two gun positions	
FORCEVILLE	18th-19th	9.30am	Bde HQ Col. move to HARPONVILLE	
MARTINSART	20th		B/154 clearing field of fire reclaiming ARCS of fire, registering.	
"	21st		C/154 sniper & mixed position in NO MAN'S LAND as night lines	
"	22nd	9.20pm	C/154 supported a demonstration on left of zone when 32nd Division carried out a raid fired 140 rounds	
"	23rd		Quiet day	
"	24,25		C/154 visited seven targets with aeroplane	
"	26,27,28		Hostile aeroplane very active, otherwise very quiet. B/154 registered when C/154 was not firing	
"	29th	11.30pm 4.12.30pm	C/154 fires 300 rounds to/154 276 rounds in support & raid by 29th Division	
"	30th		Quiet day	
"	"		II/154 in trouble all the month in preparing new gun positions	

F.C. Johnston
LT. COL. COMDG.
154 BRIGADE R.F.A.

WAR DIARY or INTELLIGENCE SUMMARY

Army Form C. 2118

MAY — Vol 5

XXXVI — 154" Bde RGA
Col H. Campbell Johnston RGA Comdg

Place	Date MAY	Hour	Summary of Events and Information	Remarks and references to Appendices
MARTINSART FORCEVILLE	1st–20th		B/154 C/154 in action under normal conditions in AVELUY WOOD. D/154 in resort preparing gun positions in AVELUY WOOD.	
	21st mid-day		On arrival of the recuperation of R Divisional Artillery and 3 mixed Brigades (3 18pdrs + 1 How.), 1 Field Gun Brigade (R 154, Bde) the designations of the former 154 Bde was changed as under:—	
			B/154 becomes C/A REID-SCOTT Comdg became II/173	
			C/154 " Capt C.T. CARTRAE " II/153	
			D/154 " Capt C.J. NEWCOMBE " II/172	
			II/172 Capt H.H. GALE Comdg became A/154	
			II/173 Capt A.H. BURNE D.S.O. " B/154	
			II/153 Capt A.H. S^MITH " C/154	
			The change was only one of nomenclature involving no personnel, horses, guns, or equipment were exchanged, the various gun positions were occupied the batteries remained in the same group.	
			3/154 E C ROSE joined from 154 Bde Am Col to A/154. Battery supplied with Ammunition Column duties from 2AC	
HARPONVILLE	22			
	24 26		Pte John B.A.C.'s and personnel rejoined including LT H.A. HOWES. Details Y. 36 T.M. Bty L. BERESFORD Comdg attached to 154 Bde RGA 2nd Armament of R eclipse of THE ROYAL REGT OF ARTILLERY.	
MESNIL MARTINSART	21st 31st		A/154, B/154, C/154 in action under normal conditions	

JC John Franco LtCol OC 154 Bde RGA

36
July
Vol 7

Army Form C. 2118

WAR DIARY or INTELLIGENCE SUMMARY

(Erase heading not required.)

154th Brigade R.F.A.
Lt. Colonel F. Campbell Johnston, R.F.A. Commanding.

Place	Date	Hour	Summary of Events and Information	Remarks and references to Appendices
JULY				
MESNIL.	1st		A/154, B/154, C/154 supported General attack by 36th (Ulster) Division	
"	2nd-6th		" Covered THIEPVAL WOOD sector of British front during 1st Army	
			operations reductions.	
"	6th		C/154 left MESNIL for ALBERT.	
"	"		B/154 moved to position 200x S. of AUTHUILE.	
THIEPVAL WOOD	4th		TRENCH MORTAR Batteries attached 154 Bde withdrawn and position L. AVELUY WOOD	
AVELUY WOOD	8th		" " " " " prior to HARPONVILLE to refit.	
MESNIL.	9th		A/154 handed over gun position to A/248 Bde R.F.A. Proceeded to wagon lines	
			in HEDAUVILLE WOOD, where Battery received orders not to proceed. Guns	
ALBERT.	7th		C/154 (Littledale) took up position near BECOURT WOOD. Registration attempted	
			L. A/63 Bde R.F.A.	
"	7th-10th		C/154 in action	
"	10th		C/154 moved to position covering sketched at OVILLERS LA BOISELLE.	
"	12th		B/154 withdrawn out of action in CHAPES SPUR North of BECOURT WOOD. Proceeded gun positions.	
FORCEVILLE.	14th		B.M.Q. Staff marched to AUTHUILE where they were joined by A/154, B/154 & C/154.	
AUTHUILE	15th		Brigade marched from AUTHUILE to CONCHY SUR CACHES.	
CONCHY.	16th		" " " CONCHY-SPASMES to MONCHY-CAYEUX.	
MONCHY.	17th		" " " MONCHY-CAYEUX to DELETTE.	
DELETTE.	18th		" " " DELETTE to CLERQUES.	
CLERQUES.	19th	6.30pm	" " " CLERQUES to ST. OMER.	
ST. OMER.	20th		" " " ST. OMER to COURTE CROIX near FLETRES.	
COURTE CROIX.	21st		" " " COURTE CROIX - C/154 to wagon line at LOCRE. B.H.Q. at BRULOOZ	
WULVERGHEM	"	10pm	A/154 went into action taking over position from C/109 Bde. R.F.A.	
"	22nd		B/154 " " in new position covering 50th Divisional front	
			B/154 made position 200x further W. covering R. DOUVE.	
	27		A/154 & B/154 in action under normal trench warfare conditions	
"	22,23,31st		B.H.Q. made from BRULOOZ near LOCRE to S.23.a.7.6. Refilled 2.5m (near NEUVE EGLISE)	
LOCRE	31st		C/154 remain at wagon line.	

F. C. Johnston
LT. COL. COMDG.
154 BRIGADE R.F.A.

WAR DIARY

INTELLIGENCE SUMMARY

Army Form C. 2118

VOL 8

154th Bde R.F.A.
Lt. Col. F.C. Johnston R.F.A.
Comdg.

Place	Date	Hour	Summary of Events and Information	Remarks and references to Appendices
PLOEGSTEERT	AUGUST 1st-5th		A/154 in action in divered Battery Position. Did not fire during this period.	
WULVERGHEM	" 1st		B/154 " " " " " "	
	" 2nd			
	" 3rd		C/154 remain at wagon lines at T.13.a.8.1.	
WHITE GATES	" 3rd		New Right Group Constituted. Consisting of 143 Bde & B/154 under command of Col. W.C. Crawford R.A. Crossing line from LA PETITE DOUVE FARM to BLACK SHED.	
	" 15th		C/154 took over guns of A/154 at Position near WHITE GATES, the latter going into action night of 14/15, remaining in action night of 15/16.	
	" 5th		A/154 took over guns from C/154 at wagon lines	
	" 12		A/154 (Reynolds) took over A/153's Position. A/154 (Royd Position) taking over from A/153 night of 11/12.	
	" 12		B/154 with battery fired 25 rounds at range of 3400 with retaliating shells.	
	" 16		B/154 Come out of action. Fired at wagon lines.	
	" 16		C/154 wagon lines moved to L.S. of DRANOUTRE.	
DRANOUTRE	" 16		C/154 Coml and Section moved into action withdrawn night of 16/17, remaining in action night of 17/18	
"	" 16-18		B/154 wagon lines moved to L.S. of DRANOUTRE.	
"	" 17		Lt. R. LLOYD THOMPSON. RFA reported sick & L. Command A/153.	
"	" 18		2/Lt H. ABBOT joined b/154 15th & from 173 Bde RFA.	
	" 19		No 27125 CARDER. F. Y/36 TM 13th sent by horse aircraft.	
	" 20	1.15am	RHQ camp at S.23.a.9.6 bombed by hostile aircraft. 3 bombs dropped wounding Nos UNWIN, Gnr HILL, Riding 3 horses wounding b/154 (Sappers). advanced into action at N.15.a.9.9. taking over form a section 13th Canadian Bdy.	
	" 23/24	Midn		
	" 24		B/154 " C/154 (Right section) " " N.15.a.9.9.". N.16.a.4.8 respectively	
	" 24/25	"	B/154 & C/154 included in RIGHT Group of the 1st Canadian Division Controlled by Colonel RAINSFORD-HANNAY. L.C. Group Consists of 3 Batteries 89th Bde (C.F.A) & B/154 & C/154 RFA. The front covered being from VIERSTRAAT - WYCHAETE Road to DIEPENBEEK - BEEK.	
	" 26		B/154 fired at damaged hostile M.G. emplacement revealed pumping apparatus.	
WULVERGHEM	" 27		A/154 Guns at action under No moment.	
	" 28		No 99.577 Gnr HARVEY. R. A/154 killed by shell fire mode laying wire from thinthe G.O.P.	
	" 29		B/154 fired in 3 rounds in retaliation for hostile T.M's.	
			No 30462 Gnr STOCKWELL. A.E. Y/36 TM 11th killed by shell fire at COURT DREVE FARM.	

F.C. Johnston
LT. COL. COMDG.
154 BRIGADE R.F.A.

w0951stray1NNN